GROWING GREAT MINDS III

The Responsibility, the Support, and the
Importance of PARENT INVOLVEMENT

Dr. Elaine S. McGhee

Diligence Publishing Company
Bloomfield, New Jersey

GROWING GREAT MINDS III

To contact the author email:

eeartdr@aol.com

GROWING GREAT MINDS III

ISBN: 979-8-9869173-5-1

Printed in the United States

TABLE OF CONTENTS

DEDICATION

With unconditional love, *"unconditional love is one of the most powerful and healing gifts given to others,"* I dedicate this book to my son Darren, my daughter Elissa, and my granddaughter Shaniah.

(What y'all want?)
Unconditional Love (no doubt)
Talking bout the stuff that don't wear off
It don't fade
It'll last for all these crazy days
These crazy nights
Whether you wrong or right
I'm a still love you
Still feel you
Still there for you
No matter what (he he)
You will always be in my heart
With unconditional love.
(Tupac Shakur)

I thank you, Darren, Elissa, and Shaniah for your support and endorsement. You are very special to me in every way as you continue encouraging me with each passing day. Because of your kindness and the amazing family that you are, I am blessed to have you as a part of my life. Whatever you do today and every day of your lives, always remember one thing: I pledge this symbol to you and will forever LOVE YOU with unconditional LOVE. And I love you in the same way He loved us. Jesus loved us unconditionally.

ACKNOWLEDGEMENTS

I acknowledge and give special thanks to all of my parents who enrolled and endorsed their children to attend my quality childcare center, known as "Kiddie Garden Learning Academy." There are not enough words to express how grateful I am for your enthusiastic participation, support, and understanding.

In particular, I acknowledge the parents of <u>my first three children</u> who took part in our childcare services and entrusted their children to us as infants. I must repeat that I thank you for your blessings and keeping the lines of communication open and positively flowing.

At the writing of this book, the three children are now nine years old, in grade four, and remain academically, emotionally, physically, and socially successful. I am filled with gratitude for parents like you three who helped us at the center to make your children happy, charming, and different kinds of flowers. Altogether, they will make this world a beautiful garden.

The best lessons were not only from the books,
but from our hearts.

"If you could look into my heart,
how *quickly you would see*
the special place you and your child hold there,
and how much you all mean to me."
(Ron Trammer)

THANK YOU PARENTS! Thank you for your help, support, encouragement, and commitment. This allowed us to provide the impact made in your children's lives. and to assist in shaping them to be the kind, respectable, individuals you are proud of.

WHAT A PARENT IS

Being a parent is being there through the
tantrums,
the milestones, and the tears,
Being a parent means that you love that little
person which you created,
more than you could ever love yourself or
anybody else!
You'd readily lose sleep
to comfort them from their nightmares,
You would risk your own life for that small
person,
you'd surely die to save them
if you needed to. Being a parent is never a
burden, it's loving somebody else
wholeheartedly and unconditionally,
for eternity!
Being a parent to your child is not a job,
It's a privilege, cherish it!
(Pinterest)

Congratulations! You are that parent.

ENDORSEMENT

This third installment of pouring into our children from Dr. Elaine S. McGhee is undoubtedly a "Pearl of Great Price!"

In Matthew 13, the "Pearl of Great Price" is the KINGDOM OF HEAVEN. Jesus Christ sacrificed HIS LIFE, so that humanity would have access to the "Pearl of Great Price" (Kingdom of Heaven).

Dr. McGhee in all of her literary triumphs, has given parents, children, employees, and future daycare operators access to this Pearl of Great Price in the field of Growing Great Minds AKA child development. In other words, Dr. McGhee sacrificed much for this "Pearl of Great Price," so that all concerned could gain access to the Kingdom of Growing Great Minds.

Because of Dr. McGhee's literary genius and experience in childcare, she has paid dearly for this "Pearl of Great Price!" She has ushered in a new era in child development.

Kudos, mysista4life. The kingdom of child development is worth any amount of sacrifice. Whatever is lost in pursuit of the kingdom of child development is a small price to pay, considering

the value of what is gained. "My good and faithful servant, well done." Matthew 25:21 KJV
You Brother In Christ

Your Brotha4Life,
Rev. D. Jerome Gourdine

ABOUT THE BOOK

My incentive for writing this book is to advise parents to become more involved in their child's education and learning more than ever. WHY? Because they will then be assured that their children will receive all the support they need to develop a positive network of what's happening at school and what can take place at home.

My message to you is an appeal to you to make certain that you, as parents, are in harmony with other pillars of support, guidance, and love. It is also my purpose to make it clear how much parents really, really, matter, as well as to make sure that parents understand that education is the process of learning, developing skills, and attaining success in life. At the same time, in this book, I strive vigorously to lead parents to be involved. Parents, you are also to be reminded that learning and "Education is too important to be left solely to educators." (Francis Keppe)

Let's also not forget that a parent's involvement and participation can benefit their children in the areas of academics, achievement, and behavior. It leads to great accomplishments. It's important to "Trust the Journey." It is undeniable that parents are responsible for every detail of their children's lives from potty training to eating fruits, meat, and vegetables. I am encouraging parents to continue or begin taking a role in their child's learning. Parents have been teaching speech, skills, and manners since their children were infants. Knowledge is what your child knows, while education is how they learn what they know. Children are the future of our world, so make education significant for them.

REMEMBER THAT:

"Education is the passport to the future, for tomorrow belongs to those who prepare for it today."
(Malcolm X)

INTRODUCTION

Children are to be looked upon as a blessing, not a burden! They are a gift from God, and the biblical role of a parent is "to be a good steward of the children God has placed into their care." When you become a parent, you take on a role unlike any other. Parenting is not for everybody. 'It changes your life. Especially when the children are little' (Toni Amos).

Parents are among the most important people in the lives of young children and being a parent is the most important privilege they'll ever have. It is like growing a garden: plant seeds, see what grows.

Many things will grow in that garden, but the unexpected will happen, and it's not always a bad thing. The unexpected can often be beautiful and magnificent. As parents watch their children grow, they wonder what their lives will be like. They try to envision the type of people they would like their children to become.

The parent's role includes meeting their children's needs from birth into adulthood, in an environment of love, support, nurturance, encouragement, direction, and guidance. A parent's heart is the key to success, and their heart is a ribbon that ties their children's future together. The word "parent" carries a broad definition and range of responsibilities, because parents lead by example. "There is no such thing as a perfect parent, so just be a real one" (Sue Atkins).

However, in spite of the imperfections of parents, Colossians 3:20 says, "Children, obey your parents, for this pleases the Lord."

One must decide if every child deserves parents, because not all parents deserve children.

It is my inspiration to help parents impart a quality learning experience and to advocate for both parents and their children to be loved.

As parents raise their children, they are responsible for assuring that their children receive the academic enrichment they need by attending a high-quality childcare center and advancing through the four stages of tutelage – pre-school, primary, secondary, and higher, as well as preparing them to live a happy and successful life. Just don't raise your children to have more than you had. It is recommended that you raise them to be more than you ever were. Parents send their children to school expecting teachers to do the complete job of educating them. This should not release parents from their responsibility. Parents have a vital role to play in their children's education. Some parents believe that school is where all the learning takes place. And some parents are of the opinion that their lack of expertise or ability to do an adequate job at home is null and void. It is my hope that parents who feel this way will gain confidence in becoming satisfactory educators after reading my book.

Dear PARENTS: At the end of the day, the most overwhelming key to your child's success is the positive involvement of you. (Jane D. Hull)

Raising children is very important, but it is a very complicated endeavor and there is no one strategy for doing it right. Inevitably, parents will not be in control of every aspect of their children's lives. The famous proverb, "It takes a village to raise a child" means that an entire community of people must provide for the children what they need to experience and grow in a safe and healthy environment (Wikipedia).

We have LOST the village. WOW! Ask yourself, "Does it take a village to raise children?"

People have moved many miles away. Some are busy working to survive. It's difficult to ask others to help raise your children. Folks are very independent thinkers, and making decisions is difficult for others. A secure attachment between children and their parents will help promote their development.

At the end of the day, the most overwhelming key to your child's success is the positive involvement of his or her parents.

AND...

I encourage you not to Worry about anything, just Pray about everything!

Now take a look at this:

Bandage scraped knees, kiss away any fears,
Watch heartbreak and dry their tears.
Teach them to know what's right
and what's wrong,

Show them how to be gentle and when
they should be strong.
Tell them you love them, and then let it show.
That's the easiest part of helping them grow.
There needs to be discipline, but don't overdo it.
Praise and encouragement strengthen their
spirit.
Show them respect for their feelings and
thoughts.
They should know they're important, self-worth
can't be bought.
Show them some patience and always be kind.
Developing minds make mistakes time to time.
Teach them to be the best they can be.
When they're happy within,
WHAT A RIDE LIFE CAN BE! (Wanda Oleson)

Can you relate? You are the parent,
so take the wheel!

CHAPTER 1

The 3 P's... Policies And Procedures For Parents

"The capacity to care...gives life its
deepest meaning and significance."
(Pablo Casals)

After parents have selected a high-quality childcare center with an effective staff for their children to attend, they have additional challenges to face in order to experience peace. Parents might not realize how important it is to be knowledgeable of policies and procedures that support their child's health, safety, learning, and playtime as priorities.

A policy is a set of rules or guidelines for the childcare center to follow in order to achieve compliance. Policies answer questions about what staff does, when, and why they do it. It is not the law!

The procedure is the instruction on how the policy is followed. Parents might not realize how important it is to have policies and procedures. This is what happens when policies and procedures are in place: expectations are set, staff is kept accountable, and they ensure compliance with the law, defense against claims, and knowledge of where to turn for help. Together, policies and procedures provide a roadmap for day-to-day operations which ensures compliance with rules, regulations and guidance in decision-making.

In New Jersey, parents can obtain or review:

CHAPTER 52 MANUAL OF REQUIREMENTS FOR CHILD CARE CENTERS. Ask and it shall be made available.

(A copy of the cover along with pages 1 and 2 of Information To Parents is provided at the end of this chapter.)

Of the twenty-two written policies, parents should be familiar with all of them, but I will only expound on one which I feel is essential and relative to all of the children.

POLICY:

Attendance – It is very important that children come to school <u>every day</u>, and <u>on time</u>, and <u>regularly.</u> It will get them in the habit and/routine they need to adopt for school.

PROCEDURE:

Parents- will call the center to inform the staff before 8:00 a.m. that their child will be absent for the day and/or if their child will be late. (A reason would be very appreciated.)

Clothing in child's cubby
Have staff place your child's other items i.e., juice, food, in refrigerator

Departure – Sign out
Check for any messages from teacher

Child Care Staff – Phone parents of students who have missed 3 days or more to establish reason for absences

The twenty-two Policies and Procedures covered in the Manual of Requirements in the childcare centers in New Jersey are listed below:

1. Activities
2. Attendance
3. Child and Staff Responsibilities
4. Clothing
5. Communication
6. Diapering and Toilet
7. Discipline
8. Emergency Preparedness
9. Fees
10. Health, Safety, Nutrition, Allergy
11. Immunization
12. Incidents
13. Late Pick Up
14. Medication
15. Missing Child
16. Napping
17. No Smoking
18. Opening/Closing
19. Program (Structure)
20. Staffing Ratios
21. Treatment of Children
22. Walks and Field Trips

CHAPTER 52

MANUAL OF REQUIREMENTS

FOR CHILD CARE CENTERS

STATE OF NEW JERSEY
DEPARTMENT OF CHILDREN AND FAMILIES

EFFECTIVE December 20, 2023

EXPIRES December 20, 2030

DEPARTMENT OF CHILDREN AND FAMILIES
OFFICE OF LICENSING
PO BOX 717
TRENTON, NEW JERSEY 08625-0717
Toll - Free Telephone 1-877-667-9845

Department of Children and Families
Office of Licensing

INFORMATION TO PARENTS

Under provisions of the _Manual of Requirements for Child Care Centers (N.J.A.C. 3A:52)_, every licensed child care center in New Jersey must provide to parents of enrolled children written information on parent visitation rights, State licensing requirements, child abuse/neglect reporting requirements and other child care matters. The center must comply with this requirement by reproducing and distributing to parents and staff this written statement, prepared by the Office of Licensing, Child Care & Youth Residential Licensing, in the Department of Children and Families. In keeping with this requirement, the center must secure every parent and staff member's signature attesting to his/her receipt of the information.

Our center is required by the State Child Care Center Licensing law to be licensed by the Office of Licensing (OOL), Child Care & Youth Residential Licensing, in the Department of Children and Families (DCF). A copy of our current license must be posted in a prominent location at our center. Look for it when you're in the center.

To be licensed, our center must comply with the Manual of Requirements for Child Care Centers (the official licensing regulations). The regulations cover such areas as: physical environment/life-safety; staff qualifications, supervision, and staff/child ratios; program activities and equipment; health, food and nutrition; rest and sleep requirements; parent/community participation; administrative and record keeping requirements; and others.

Our center must have on the premises a copy of the Manual of Requirements for Child Care Centers and make it available to interested parents for review. If you would like to review our copy, just ask any staff member. Parents may view a copy of the Manual of Requirements on the DCF website at http://www.nj.gov/dcf/providers/licensing/laws/CCCmanual.pdf or obtain a copy by sending a check or money order for $5 made payable to the "Treasurer, State of New Jersey", and mailing it to: NJDCF, Office of Licensing, Publication Fees, PO Box 657, Trenton, NJ 08646-0657.

We encourage parents to discuss with us any questions or concerns about the policies and program of the center or the meaning, application or alleged violations of the Manual of Requirements for Child Care Centers. We will be happy to arrange a convenient opportunity for you to review and discuss these matters with us. If you suspect our center may be in violation of licensing requirements, you are entitled to report them to the Office of Licensing toll free at 1 (877) 667-9845. Of course, we would appreciate your bringing these concerns to our attention, too.

Our center must have a policy concerning the release of children to parents or people authorized by parents to be responsible for the child. Please discuss with us your plans for your child's departure from the center.

Our center must have a policy about administering medicine and health care procedures and the management of communicable diseases. Please talk to us about these policies so we can work together to keep our children healthy.

Our center must have a policy concerning the expulsion of children from enrollment at the center. Please review this policy so we can work together to keep your child in our center.

Parents are entitled to review the center's copy of the OOL's Inspection/Violation Reports on the center, which are available soon after every State licensing inspection of our center. If there is a licensing complaint

Investigation, you are also entitled to review the OOL's Complaint Investigation Summary Report, as well as any letters of enforcement or other actions taken against the center during the current licensing period. Let us know if you wish to review them and we will make them available for your review or you can view them online at https://childcareexplorer.niccs.com/portal/.

Our center must cooperate with all DCF inspections/investigations. DCF staff may interview both staff members and children.

Our center must post its written statement of philosophy on child discipline in a prominent location and make a copy of it available to parents upon request. We encourage you to review it and to discuss with us any questions you may have about it.

Our center must post a listing or diagram of those rooms and areas approved by the OOL for the children's use. Please talk to us if you have any questions about the center's space.

Our center must offer parents of enrolled children ample opportunity to assist the center in complying with licensing requirements; and to participate in and observe the activities of the center. Parents wishing to participate in the activities or operations of the center should discuss their interest with the center director, who can advise them of what opportunities are available.

Parents of enrolled children may visit our center at any time without having to secure prior approval from the director or any staff member. Please feel free to do so when you can. We welcome visits from our parents.

Our center must inform parents in advance of every field trip, outing, or special event away from the center, and must obtain prior written consent from parents before taking a child on each such trip.

Our center is required to provide reasonable accommodations for children and/or parents with disabilities and to comply with the New Jersey Law Against Discrimination (LAD), P.L 1945, c. 169 (N.J.S.A. 10:5-1 et seq.), and the Americans with Disabilities Act (ADA), P.L 101-336 (42 U.S.C. 12101 et seq.). Anyone who believes the center is not in compliance with these laws may contact the Division on Civil Rights in the New Jersey Department of Law and Public Safety for information about filing an LAD claim at (609) 292-4605 (TTY users may dial 711 to reach the New Jersey Relay Operator and ask for (609) 292-7701), or may contact the United States Department of Justice for information about filing an ADA claim at (800) 514-0301 (voice) or (800) 514-0983 (TTY).

Our center is required, at least annually, to review the Consumer Product Safety Commission (CPSC) unsafe children's products list, ensure that items on the list are not at the center, and make the list accessible to staff and parents and/or provide parents with the CPSC website at https://www.cpsc.gov/Recalls. Internet access may be available at your local library. For more information call the CPSC at (800) 638-2772.

Anyone who has reasonable cause to believe that an enrolled child has been or is being subjected to any form of hitting, corporal punishment, abusive language, ridicule, harsh, humiliating or frightening treatment, or any other kind of child abuse, neglect, or exploitation by any adult, whether working at the center or not, is required by State law to report the concern immediately to the *State Central Registry Hotline, toll free at (877) NJ ABUSE/(877) 652-2873*. Such reports may be made anonymously. Parents may secure information about child abuse and neglect by contacting: DCF, Office of Communications and Legislation at (609) 292-0422 or go to www.state.nj.us/dcf/.

CHAPTER 2

Parent's Involvement In Their Child's School Life

New York, New York—It's so nice they named it twice. This chapter is so nice, the issues are stated twice to highlight the parent's partnerships and importance in their child's school life.

As a parent, participation in your child's school life is the cornerstone of their upbringing. You are your child's first teacher, so we are going to take a deep dive and read about how a parent's involvement affects their child's education. By the way, involvement does not just mean dropping off or picking up your child from school. There should be much more. Involvement is a broad term that takes much more configuration both inside and outside of school.

Involvement at <u>home</u> includes:

- Help with homework.

- Model desired behavior.
- Provide continuous commitment.
- Monitor completion of homework.
- Provide a space and time for homework.

Involvement at <u>school</u> includes:

- Communication with teachers.
- Volunteering for school activities.
- Attending parent-teacher conferences.

"Parental Involvement, in most any form, produces measurable gains in student achievement." (Armendia Dixon)

Academic success does not just rest in letter grades, and letter grades don't really measure success. The following are also factors in a child's success:

Attendance – arrive on time and always present.
Attitude – not in a good mood all of the time.
A's grades - are important.
Appearance – first impressions are lasting ones (it's how you are perceived).

There are <u>many</u> more factors that contribute to the role that parents play in their children's lives academically, socially, mentally, and physically that can affect a child's academic success:

PROVERBS 22.6 *Train up a child the way he should go and when he is old, he will not depart from it.*

IN THE CLASSROOM *"A teacher is a compass that activates the magnets of curiosity, knowledge and wisdom in the pupil." (children)* (Ever Garrison)

Some Additional Factors include:

Love of learning	Passion to learn
Curiosity	Intelligence
Early educational milestones	Pubertal development
Learning to read	Setting a schedule
Reading ability	Staying on track
Participation	Self-esteem
Personality	Having faith

Socio-economic status	Early school progression
Confidence	Reach milestones
Don't multi-task	Study environment
Getting along	Focus
Organized	Home instruction

LET'S MAKE A DEAL – *So parents, what role do you want to play in Your child's school life???*

Parents, here is how you can have an impact on your child's school life:

a) Learn together.
b) Present yourself as a role model.
c) Make everyday activities educational.
d) Try supplemental activities.
e) Join a parent group.
f) Monitor your child's schoolwork.
g) Keep lines of communication open.
h) Prioritize parent-teacher conferences
i) Volunteer at your child's school.
j) Read to and with your child.
k)

"There is no elevator to success.
You have to take the stairs."
(Zig Ziglar)

AND

"You don't have to see the whole staircase,
Just take the <u>first step.</u>"
(Martin Luther King, Jr.)

Why is there a "lack" of parent involvement in your child's school life?

Unfortunately, parents, our children's education appears or seems as though it has become a pastime rather than a priority because of the absence of activity and respectfully loud boisterous parents, NOT GOOD! It is time for parents to SUPPORT and get involved in their child's education.

"Behind every child who
believes in him/her self
is a parent
who believed
first."
(Matthew Jacobson)

Well, parents, how can we turn this around????

- After checking your child's yearly calendar, plan to schedule around important dates, be available to attend and arrange for childcare.

- Check in with your child's teacher, to ask questions about your child's progress and behavior.

- Develop positive relationships with the school's staff

- Take an interest in your child's schoolwork

- Communicate with your child about what they are learning, i.e., "What did you learn today in school?"

REMEMBER. Together, <u>Teachers,</u> <u>Parents,</u> and <u>Children</u> are all a part of this educational journey.

"Parent involvement" can be a valuable tool to determine the success of a child in school.

When parents participate, they're showing concern. The message to the children is that it's important to learn.

Parental support can be shown in many different ways. Volunteering, serving on committees, or joining the P.T.A, attending "open house" and events like "Back to School Night" are all a part of fulfilling your role as a parent and should become the rule.

The parent stays connected and demonstrates respect... encouraging words and guidance is what your child expects!

Parents and teachers together form a most popular team when they work together. It helps the child's self-esteem.

"So the level of "parent involvement" becomes an accurate sign – A more important factor in education would be most difficult to find! (Coach Akren)

Parents Get Involved – School is Cool.

The 10 Commandments for Parents

Responsibilities

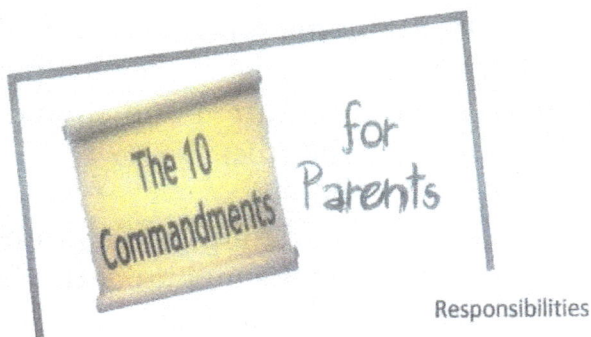

1. Provide protection for your children from all hurt, harm, and danger.

2. Provide your children with food, clothing, and a place to live.

3. Provide financial support for your children.

4. Provide safety, supervision, and control of your children.

5. Provide medical care for your children.

6. Provide a quality education for your children.

7. Provide more encouragement and less criticism for your children.

8. Provide encouraging dialogues with your children.

9. Provide more emphasis on moral values and less emphasis on materialistic things.

10. Provide more quality time for your children.

ABCs of Parenting
(Leah Davies)

Accept and value yourself and your children.

Be consistent, honest, fair, but firm as you relate to your child.

Concentrate on what you like about your children and comment on it.

Develop interests of your own.

Encourage your child to discuss ideas and goals, expressing the belief that they can do many things well.

Forgive your child's mistakes which are a natural part of learning.

Gladly share your time, affection, and support.

Help your child feel safe and secure.

Interest your child in work by complimenting their efforts.

Joyfully take pleasure in your child's life.

Keep harsh criticisms to yourself, avoid using "should" and "ought."

Let your child experience the results of their behavior.

Model by positive example those qualities you want your child to have.

Negotiate privileges and responsibilities, never avoid overindulgence.

Offer some choices, allowing your child to make decisions.

Problem-solve with your child, listen carefully to their thoughts and feelings.

Quit blaming, shaming, and threatening.

Respect your child's right to grow at their own pace without being pushed or compared to others.

Share household tasks among all family members so that your child makes a contribution and feels a sense of belonging.

Take time to read with your child, thus instilling a love of books and learning.

Use a photo album to record pleasant family memories.

Value honesty, kindness, dependability, truthfulness, and caring.

Weather trials together as a family.

X eXamine your attitude toward your children.

Yield to professional advice concerning healthy living habits.

Zestfully participate in a variety of family traditions and activities.

CHAPTER 3

Become A <u>Great</u> Coaching Parent For <u>Your</u> Child

YOU GOT THIS!

'A <u>good</u> coach can change a game. A <u>great</u> coach can change a life.'

Coaching as a parent can have a positive and negative impact on your child. So, slow your roll parents. How does it work? Stay in your lane. This means when you are coaching, be only a coach, but when you are a parent in your home, be just that – the parent! It is important that you establish <u>clear</u> boundaries.

You will find that coaching your child can be a great experience when handled well, not only for you as the parent, but for your child too! Also, coaching will strengthen your relationship with your child. The role you undertake as a coaching parent to assist with your child's academic

41

success should not have stopped when you enrolled them into a quality childcare center. Why not? Because coaching will be a method of enhancing and developing skills to inspire a lifelong love of learning for your child. Wow! What a great opportunity. But what has 'love' got to do with it? Love is an invitation to perfection and a constant invitation to "show up, speak up, and lift up" your child.

Parents, how can you coach your child's learning? First create an environment that encourages learning. It should include everything that is a part of the plan for instruction. Namely, what your child will learn and how they will learn it.

An inquisitive child is usually the best learner, but they must ALL be encouraged to ask the Questions: **WHO, WHAT, WHEN, WHERE, and WHY?**

Here is how you can coach your child's learning:

Talk with your child often: use sentences, avoid baby talk, see things from your child's point of view, permit them to talk to you about feelings, i.e., anger, fear.

Promote creativity: sing songs together, give them musical toys, paints, molding clay, (for gifts). *Don't spend too much money.*

Introduce a "love" for books: let your children see you reading. (They love to imitate you.) read to your child often. (Answer and ask questions about the story.)

Encourage your child: support your child with approval as they try something new. (Let them know you made mistakes too.)

Discipline with love: use a positive approach, set clear limits, be reasonable and consistent.

Show love often: show affection, care, comfort, concern, nurture, support.

As a coaching parent, also be aware of the negative and positive impacts you can have on your child. "Young people need models not critics." (John Wooden)

Some Negative Impacts

> Being harder on your child

> ➤ More apt to lose your temper on your child
> ➤ Set higher expectations for your child
> ➤ Have difficulty separating your roles

Some Positive Impacts

> ➤ Being enthusiastic
> ➤ Being trusting and supportive
> ➤ Being observant, patient and clear
> ➤ Having a positive attitude

This parenting journey of coaching can vary and that is why I decided to have you think about designing a path to encompass The 4 C's of Coaching:

Character/Caring   Confidence

Competence   Connection

AND

The ABC's of Coaching:

Accountability

Belief in the coach.

Conversation

(Dr Kim Grengs)

As a coaching parent, you can be one of the pieces to your child's future. Every parent understands the challenges and rewards of teaching children.

Here are some additional tips on <u>how</u> to coach:

    a. Use appropriate strategies.
    b. Plan a great practice.
    c. Keep the children safe.
    d. Make it fun.
    e. Use methods to help them grow and learn.
    f. Engage with your child's teacher.

Oh! Let's not forget the 'steps to coaching':

WARM UP, MOVE FORWARD, WRAP IT UP.

Yes parents, keep it 'Short and Sweet.'

"Coaching is unlocking one's potential to
maximize their growth."
(John Whitmore)

Encourage your child:
Support your child with approval because often
they try something new.
(Let them know you made mistakes too).

Show love often.

Now, how can coaching parents help with the
curriculum? The curriculum is a course of study
used in both early childhood education and
kindergarten through grade 12 and used in
reference to knowledge and skills the children are
expected to learn. The curriculum includes
specific learning standards, lessons,
assignments, and materials used to organize and
to teach a particular course/class (Tom Vander
Ark). It is also a guide that can be used by
coaching parents to help their child to achieve
success along the path of their rigorous academic
journey. The curriculum should include goals,

methods, materials, and assignments. The ideas that can help you include the following:

READING and WRITING:
- Play writing games.
- Make up rhymes.
- Provide books and magazines.
- Write your notes.
- Get a library card for your child.

MATH:
- Play games using numbers, i.e., bingo, dominos.
- Figure out things, i.e., temperature degrees, how it drops and rises.

SOCIAL STUDIES:
- Educational gifts to test history and geography. i.e., puzzles, maps.
- Recognize national holidays (school is usually closed).
- Visit museums or parades. (school is usually closed).

SCIENCE:
- Let your child plant seeds and grow some plants.
- Allow them to collect leaves, rocks, or insects, describe and name them.

- Work together to build something, i.e., house, car.
- Talk about and describe the four seasons, i.e., winter, spring, summer, and fall.

Parents, as coaches, you can bring out the "GREAT" student in your child. The most important years of their life are birth to age three. Be warm, loving and responsive. Talk, read, hum, or sing to your child. Every child can learn, just not on the same day or in the same way.

(The Montessori Message)

CHAPTER 4

The 5 W's and 1 H of Parent and Teacher Relationships

WHO: *Parents and Teachers*

Positive parent and teacher relationships are crucial for a child's learning success, and the relationship needs to be established early! There is an urgency to work hand in hand for the best learning experience results. Just as parents can learn from teachers, teachers can learn from parents.

> Together we may give
> our children the roots
> to grow and the wings
> to fly.
> (Pinterest)

WHAT: *Relationships*

The relationship of parents and teachers is when they <u>work</u> together through the 3 C's which are: *Collaborating, Communicating,* and *Consistency.*

C – Collaborating is being open to and accepting new ideas, achieving the same goal, "success in the classroom," which leads to deeper learning. Performance is improved. Personal growth is encouraged.

> Alone we can do so little;
> together we can do so much.
> (Helen Keller)

C – Communicating is a two-way communication which benefits the parents and teachers. There is a need to listen more to parent concerns. Teachers can assure parents that they have their child's best interest at heart. Some tools of communication include text messages, e-mails, phone calls, and in-person meetings. There is no one tool that works best.

> The art of conversation is
> the art of hearing as

well as being heard.
(William Hazlitt)

C – Consistency involves utilizing opportunities and experiences that are provided at school to support your child's learning that are to be "copied" at home. Parents should try to provide regular routines, and a sense of security, while understanding boundaries and what is expected of them to be carried out at school the same way it is done at home. Children are counting on us, teachers and parents, to provide consistency and structure.

All children need a little help,
a little hope,
and somebody who
believes in them.
(Magic Johnson)

The role of parents is to encourage and motivate their child, to support their child, to be positive, and to be understanding. The teacher is to nurture the children, and mold them to be learners and to be responsible. This relationship will lead to a child being positive about attending their childcare center.

Tell me and I forget,
Teach me and
I may remember.
Involve me,
and I will learn.
(Ben Franklin)

<u>WHEN</u>: The time is now!

Teachers will contact parents as soon as they know who is in their class to establish a relationship for early learning success. This relationship must be built on trust and responsibility from everyone involved. An introductory phone call at the beginning of a new school year and throughout the school year should be the focus for the task of developing trust and setting the guidelines for parent and teacher responsibility.

"A little text can have a big impact.
It can change a parent's engagement from reactive to proactive."
(Gwen Pescatore)

WHERE: **At mutual places for Parents and Teachers to meet.**

Some of the key ways and places <u>where</u> the relationships can begin are:

Back to School Nights
Parent-Teacher Conferences
Pick-up and Drop-off Times
Parent Night
Zoom
Classroom Volunteering

WHY: **For knowledge and academic success.**

If parents and teachers work as partners in a relationship, children do better in childcare and at home. Early learning success will be kept up to date. The children will feel safe. Parents working together with teachers can affect the child's attitude, absenteeism attendance, and behavior, as well as their feelings of belonging.

Example: There was a child who attended my Kiddie Garden center who was 3 years old and would or could not talk. He just always pointed to say what he wanted to say. A suggestion that he be tested was made by me. The father was in denial and continued to deny our recommendation. It was suggested at the center that the child had autism and needed outside help.

(Autism is a disorder that is characterized
by difficulty in social interaction and communication and by repetitive or restrictive patterns of thought and behavior.)

The family finally conceded and had him tested and received extra help for him. They moved away, but his grandmother, who still lives here said, "We can't keep him quiet."

Coming together is a beginning,
keeping together is progress,
working together is success.
(Henry Ford)

HOW: **To work together.**

Both parents and teachers must work together towards the same goal which is to amplify the learning experiences for each child. Making an effort to develop and provide frequent two-way communication via the following ways is needed:

> Ask questions about extra support.
> Be on same level as parents.
> Call with positive thoughts.
> Communicate often and effectively.
> Email/Text messages.
> Listen to Parents/Teachers.
> Learn names – Parents/Teachers.
> Newsletters.
> Parents dread negative information.
> Provide a survey for feedback.
> School website.
> Send "happy notes."
> Start messages with good news.
> Show gratitude "thank you."

The Parent Journey: communication, respect for and trust in teachers.

The Teaching Journey: positive relationships, respect for and flexibility with parents.

The Child's Learning Journey: early experiences and positive influences from parents and teachers significantly shape a child's development.

CHAPTER 5

The Right Time For Parents To Set Goals

Now is always the best time to set goals regardless of when now is.

But why even set goals??? Setting goals allows your child to be focused, challenged, motivated, and confident in being prepared for kindergarten and beyond, as well as ready to learn.

Goal setting can be a positive experience for you and your child together. Setting goals will also implant a sense of purpose for action and making better decisions. They will make a path to show your child how to take steps towards their end game by taking. . .baby steps, then giant steps.

Yes, setting goals should include infants, toddlers, and preschoolers. However, short goals are best. It does not matter how many you set. Completing them is what's important.

"The secret to getting ahead is getting started."

(Mark Twain)

Parents, let's get ready, get set, and GO to help your child commit to and attain the goals which you have been thinking about and have set for them. Remember to write them down, set a deadline, develop a plan, then take action! Oh, and parents, don't forget that *"goals are dreams with deadlines"* (Diana Scharf). Also, goals are a vision you have for your child. Make sure that the goals are:

Academic	Relevant
Achievable	Short Term
Realistic	Time Sensitive

I offer a few goals for preschool children, and they are:

ACADEMICS – in preparation for
kindergarten.
(It is a commitment toward
your child's education

affecting their academic
performance.)

➢ Identify child's first name in sequence:
first, middle, and last.
➢ Say their first and last name.
➢ Identify letters in child's name.
➢ Sort objects by color, shape, and size.
➢ Rote count to 10.
➢ Count objects to 100.
➢ Development Concept of time. i.e.,
breakfast, lunch, snack, potty, and nap
time.

INDEPENDENCE – also in preparation for
kindergarten. (It is to
create an expectation
toward your child's
ability affecting their
self-reliance.)

Put on coat independently.
Take care of your belongings.
Clean up (toys, materials).
Bathroom routine independently.

The goals that are set should be challenging and realistic so that they can be achieved. Short term goals are best. As I stated before, **it does not matter how many you set. Completing them is what's important.** Goal setting also implants a sense of purpose for actions, focus, and the ability to make better decisions. It will also make the path smoother for your child to achieve success in life.

You may be asking, "Well what steps do we take to set the goals?" You have to decide what you want your child to achieve and how they can try and accomplish the specific goal.

You should:

- Identify the goal you want to set for your child.

- Establish a time frame you want the goal completed.

- Think through the steps.

- Keep track of the process of the goal.

- Celebrate your child's success.

Once again, let us look at the 5W's for goal setting. Why? Because it teaches your child responsibility, how to plan, how to make better decisions, and builds confidence. Always start with the end in mind, but you must be specific. Set goals and work toward achieving them.

EXAMPLE GOAL: _You would like your child to improve their reading fluency and comprehension._

My preschool child.
Does your child want to do it?
Will your child do it?
Is the goal important for your child?

Children go through phases of reading development from preschool through third grade, from the exploration of books to independent reading. A goal will force growth in your child to want to achieve that goal and confidence that you believe they can achieve it. Let's look at the 5W's and how they can help How the 5W's can help to accomplish each goal:

WHO: You, as parent will read to your child or with your child.

WHAT: The book will be chosen from the child's reading list from school.

WHEN: You, as parent will read to your child for at least 30 minutes or more every night.

WHERE: The book will be read at home, the library, online, or on ZOOM.

WHY: To enhance your child's reading skills or ability and fluency.

Parents who set goals will give their child another focal point. With your encouragement, you will be able to inspire hidden potential in your child and will become a driving force to their success. Without any goals, your efforts to help your child will also become incoherent and often confusing. Without a goal, you will not be able to measure your child's progress toward remaining focused. AND, without a goal, you have no motivation to help your child now but will be more likely to put off tasks until tomorrow.

"Setting goals is the first step in turning the invisible into visible. (Tony Robbins)

CHAPTER 6

Parents' Understanding of Their
CHILD LEARNING THROUGH PLAY

"Play gives children a chance to practice what
they are learning." Fred Rogers)

Play is good for your child's recreational amusement and enjoyment. Your child should have full freedom to play the way they want as long as it is deemed safe. In education, "play" means "children's experiences and knowledge in order to help them create meaning, sense, and understanding." Play is not like a competitive sport. Play sets the foundation for your child to become curious and an excited learner. Children are naturally playful so "Let them play."

There is no right or wrong way to play. It allows your child to relax and\or let off steam. Play is also an activity for <u>fun</u> where children show their remarkable ability for exploration and decision making. Play is something children can do with a friend, on their own, speaking aloud, speaking silently, playing messy, or risky, playing quietly, or relaxed. They only need time and space. Whatever way children choose to play, what it comes down to or adds up to is WHEN CHILDREN PLAY, THEY LEARN.

Your child will learn best from joyful experiences that meaningfully connect to their lives, from actively engaging in allowing the testing of things, and from being socially interactive with others. Learning through play is important and can help your child to be ready for school. It will also encourage their imagination and help them with literacy and numeracy skills. (Family Lives)

There are two different types of play:

Structured

Your child will follow directions or rules.

Example: Board Game
Puzzles

Unstructured

Your child can do what interests them. Has no direction.

Example: Plays on the playground. i.e., swings
Dress up. i.e., fireman, nurse

*Your child's play will change as he/she
grows older.*

Play is designed for the little one's needs and how they will grow physically, intellectually, emotionally, and socially. Parents, the key to fun is for you to <u>join in.</u> Play arises when parents play with their child\children. Unfortunately, time spent playing has now decreased because families today are so busy. The struggle is finding time to play in between long work hours. The quality of time is very important. Your child loves playing with you. There are connections between play and your child's learning. Parents tend to doubt their child's learning aspects of play. Instead, they are focusing more on and putting more importance and emphasis on instruction, workbooks, worksheets, and children sitting in the classroom.

I am a child
I am not built to sit still,
keep my hands to myself, take
turns, stand in line, be patient
or keep quiet.

I need motion, I need novelty,
I need adventure, and I need
to engage the world with my whole body.
Let me play.
Trust me, I am learning.

Elaheh Mottahedel Bos

Parents, let's take a look at some learning examples:

Math: The children can pretend to be *cashiers* or *shoppers to use* measurements, block sizes.

Science: How much sand will it take to fill your bucket?

Social Studies:

Put on pajamas, it's bedtime – *dramatic area*

Put your arm in here so I can take an X-ray – *community helpers*

Have a package for you in my truck – *postal workers*

<u>Language:</u>

> Reading, vocabulary, speech, using the three pigs: *create an Imaginary story.* Use familiar words and what they start with, i.e., *Pizza starts with a "P".*

But parents, HERE IT IS:

Do you remember the "Good Old Days?????"

At this writing, I have some memories you may have found joyful and meaningful as <u>play</u> experiences for you:

Do you remember life before the computer?
Back when ....
Memory was something that
You lost with age
An application was for employment.
A program was a TV show.
A cursor used profanity.
A keyboard was a piano.
A web was a spider's home.
A virus was the flu.
A CD was a bank account.
A hard drive was a long trip on the road.
A mouse pad was where a mouse lived.

Do you remember?

Will your child experience the same kind of joy, meaning, and family bonding together in play and learning today that you experienced when you were a child? And, do you remember any of the lessons in the "good old days" that touched on play as well as many life lessons?

Attend church.	Play boardgames.
Be a good friend.	Remain honest.
Be quick to help.	Serve others.
Express gratitude.	Value education.
Forgive quickly.	Value family.

And let's not forget prayer, which is an important part of your child's development too!!!!! Prayer is one of the best ways to help your child focus on what's important and what really matters. In the "good old days," children "shared" toys because families were unable to afford manufactured toys. Children had to find their own way of making their fun. i.e., hoops, jump ropes, marbles, baseball cards, jigsaw puzzles, dolls, Lionel trains, yo-yos, park swings, hopscotch, checkers, chess. Children learned about themselves and the world through play. Children made most of their own decisions. They were motivated, immersed in the moment, engaged in spontaneous play (not scripted), and play was enjoyable. But, in the end, in the Good Old Days" *and* "Today," <u>PLAY</u> helps children:

> ➢ Be ready for kindergarten.
> ➢ Adjust to a school schedule and setting.
> ➢ Be ready to learn.
> ➢ Have better learning behavior.

Thank – You, God,

For feet to run.

Thank – You

FOR MY PLAY AND FUN;

For eyes to see.

For hands to lift,

For food to eat.

And every gift

That makes me strong

And wish to sing,

"Thank – You, God,

FOR EVERYTHING".

The Value of Play
(Laurie Monopoli)

You say that you love your children,
And are concerned that they learn today,
As am I, that's why I'm providing
A variety of kinds of play.

You are asking what's the value
Of having your children play?
Your daughter's creating a tower,
She may be a builder someday.

You're asking me the value
Of blocks and sand and clay.
Your children are solving problems,
They will use that skill every day.

You're saying that you don't want your son
To play in that sissy way.
He's learning to cuddle a doll,
He may be a father someday.

You're questioning the learning centers,
They just look like useless play.
Your children are making choices,
They'll be on their own someday.

You're worried your children are learning
And later they'll have to pay.
They're learning a pattern for learning,
For they'll be learners always.

71

CHAPTER 7

Parents Inspire Your Child "Love Of Learning"

"A happy life is one spent in learning, earning, and yearning." (Lillian Gish)

The 'love of learning' is universal and cannot be taught. Parents, be an advocate for your child because they are born with a natural 'love of learning' and you can make it fun. Inspiration in the life of your child, coming from you as a parent, can be converted into productivity and creativity. Don't worry about it, just pray about it. Learning is a gift and for that reason the gift lasts for a lifetime and opportunities will broaden your child's horizons.

"The capacity to learn is a gift,
The ability to learn is a skill,
The willingness to learn is a choice."
(Brian Herbet)

Parents, you can enhance and embrace learning with the right attitude. For example, if you love learning, your child will try to follow in your footsteps. "Teachers also, who love teaching, teach children to love learning." An early start to instill a love of learning in your child is recommended because you only get one chance at it. What is 'Love of Learning'? And what is it all about anyway? Parents, I thought you'd never ask.

LOVE of learning is a passion for learning, and a desire to learn just for the sake of learning and a curiosity about learning.

Curiosity is the motivating factor that takes the lead in one's seeking out new information to hold on to or enhance the information they already have. Curiosity and love of learning are closely related in intensity. It is the primary motivating factor for seeking knowledge. Parents, did you know that as babies, your children have an innate curiosity that leads them to eagerly explore the world around them and to soak up new information and skills like sponges.

Some of the ways to instill a love of learning are:

a. Read, read, and read to stimulate their minds.
b. Be enthusiastic by having them mimic you, parents.
c. Be supportive, so don't scold for not learning.
d. Be inquisitive and use your imagination.
e. Make learning fun and turn learning into a game.
f. Ask that they will share their opinion.
g. Never judge and refrain from upsetting them harshly.
h. Research together in a win/win situation.
i. Get into nature because outdoors is a very healthy opportunity.
j. Let them lead the way.
k. Let them choose and don't force them to learn.
l. Teach an adventure and involve them in the planning process.

Start early because your time is very short. I suggest that one way that you can navigate the journey of your child's love of learning is through the curriculum (which you should be acquainted with). The curriculum also matters, and to parents who are unfamiliar with the curriculum, it is what gives your child the opportunity to "freely" fall in love with the joys of learning and to experience firsthand how wonderful learning can be. As a parent, it is your task to <u>inspire</u> your child to <u>want</u> to learn and not be <u>forced</u> to learn. How??? Through nourishing and nurturing your child.

<u>Nourishing</u> will provide your child with an abundance of readiness necessary for survival and for the best chances for the love of learning and success of learning. This includes attending a quality childcare center where some of the methods already mentioned or some of the methods to follow will be practiced.

Infants from birth: They learn through their five senses and try to make sense of what's going on around them.

Look – their eyes. (seeing their parents smile)
Listen – their ears. (to sounds)
Touch – their hands. (reaching and grabbing)
Taste – their mouth. (good, want more)
Smell – their nose. (bad, turn away)

Toddlers: They learn domain-general and domain specific skills. The groundwork is laid for activities that help sensory and skill development.

Learning Language skills – Aa, Bb, Cc's
Colors
Numbers – 1, 2, 3 to 100
Early thinking skills.
Playing – Dramatics

Preschoolers: They learn to have a positive feeling about learning new things and feel autonomous. Learning takes place and is enhanced.

Gross motor skills – begins to jump
Early math concepts
Pre-writing, listening, and musical skills
Language and Vocabulary

This list is by no means complete. But your child will be <u>ready</u> for kindergarten as mine were from Kiddie Garden.

"Learning by Doing" (hands-on approach)
(John Dewey, American Philosopher)

Learning is most effective between 10:00 a.m. and 2:00 p.m. which is noted in the schedule that the children followed in my book, *"Growing Great Minds II."* It should not feel like a job or working to your child because it should be <u>fun</u>, and while having fun, you will find that the learning will 'stick.'

<u>Nurturing</u> will provide your child with a careful process through which the utmost impact is made so as to <u>ensure</u> not only <u>survival,</u> but a love for learning and <u>survival</u> along the lines of the best chances for success, like the child taking ownership of the responsibility of their education.

- Play games, i.e., matching upper and lower case letters, letter sounds, numbers and quantities, colors and color words.

- Find your child's learning style for reading and writing, i.e., visual, auditory, kinesthetic. (You should use/try all three styles to practice, retain, and fully understand.)

- Make it easy. (hide-and-seek). Hide the letters around the house or room, and as your child finds them, have them put the letters and numbers in order, i.e., C.B.D.A (ABCD), 3,1,4,2, (1234).

Parents, please remember that continuous learning is important. As long as you are alive, you will be learning new things because if you stop learning, your brain will probably stop performing.

This undertaking by you, the child's parent, and your child's teacher will set your child up and open up your child's heart to learning to achieve global success for years to come. Parents, it's easy to implement and it's really fruitful for your child to adopt 'a love for learning'.

The beautiful thing about learning, especially 'a love of learning' is that no one can take what you learn away from you. Parents you can:

"Inspire hope,

Ignite the imagination,

and

Instill a love of learning."

(Brad Henry)

WHAT Should MATTER TO YOU AS YOUR CHILD'S PARENT!

Children Learn What They Live

If a child lives with criticism – He learns to condemn.

If a child lives with hostility – He learns to fight.

If a child lives with ridicule – He learns to be shy.

If a child lives with tolerance – He learns to be patient.

If a child lives with shame – He will learn to feel guilty.

If a child lives with encouragement – He learns confidence.

If a child lives with praise – He learns to appreciate.

If a child lives with approval – He learns to like himself.

If he lives with acceptance and friendship, He learns to find love in the world.

(DL Nolte and Rachel Harris)

An Assessment Used at Kiddie Garden
to Help With Class Placements

I named these uppercase letters:	A B C D E F G H I J K L M N O P Q R S T U V W X Y Z

I named these shapes:	○		□		▭		△
	☆		○		♡		◇

I counted to...	

I named these numbers:	1	2	3	4	5
	6	7	8	9	10

I counted with 1:1 correspondence	Yes / No	Comments:

I used these positional words correctly:	Inside Over Outside Under Between Beside On

Name Formation	Yes / No	Comments:

I named these colors:	Pink Red Orange Yellow Green Blue Purple Brown Black White

I can sort by color:	Yes / No	Comments:

I can make an AB pattern:	Yes / No	Comments:

I grip my scissors correctly:	Yes / No	Comments:

Areas of Strength: Areas to Improve:

    1.   1.

    2.   2.

    3.   3.

    4.   4.

    5.   5.

Comments:

If a child can't learn the
way we teach them,
maybe we should
teach the way they learn.

CHAPTER 8

Parents Say, SAFETY FIRST

"Be Aware...Take Care"

Parents feel that a childcare center should always be a safe place for their child physically, emotionally, and mentally because, with "no safety, know pain," but with "know safety, no pain."

What is safety? It means to have all precautions in place. It is a state in which hazards and conditions leading to physical harm are controlled. Children should be provided with security and families provided with peace of mind. It is always better to avoid unnecessary risks. Many safety standards that you as parents assume to be practiced <u>are not</u> being practiced.

FLASH!
FLASH!
FLASH!

Safety is everyone's responsibility!

Parents, be aware that children getting hurt at childcare centers is a very <u>common</u> thing. i.e., *Falling.* It is the leading cause of injury. Especially during playtime, which is absolutely necessary, but parents, 'let them be children.' I'm sure you would rather be safe than sorry. Right??? Well, have you done your homework on the safety quality at your child's childcare center? In New Jersey, licensing standards <u>must</u> <u>be</u> <u>met</u> by childcare centers and you as parents should want the same. The following checklist will be helpful to determine safety practices and to make sure that the center you have chosen is as safe as it can be.

A safety checklist will confirm safety for your child. The most important rule of safety is that <u>everyone,</u> and I do mean <u>everyone</u>, follows <u>all</u> of the safety rules and regulations. The rules are in place to protect your child, other children, and staff from potential hazards.

Parent Checklist (Take it and ease your mind.)

	Yes	No
1. At least one staff member has an up-to-date CPR and first aid training.	_____	_____
2. A First Aid Kit in every room.	_____	_____
3. Licensing standards are met.	_____	_____
4. Acceptable staff-to-child ratios are met.	_____	_____
5. Space areas for the children.	_____	_____
6. Access to a nurse or health consultant.	_____	_____
7. Discipline policy.	_____	_____
8. Locked interior doors.	_____	_____
9. Cameras and monitors.	_____	_____
10. Smoke alarms and fire extinguishers.	_____	_____
11. Sign in/Sign out for visitors.	_____	_____
12. Gates at top and bottom of any stairs secured.	_____	_____
13. Toys in good condition.	_____	_____
14. Windows with guards for windows and ventilation in every classroom.	_____	_____

	Yes	No
15. Furniture and equipment in <u>good</u> condition.	_____	_____
16. All electrical outlets covered.	_____	_____
17. Exit paths remain clear.	_____	_____
18. Evacuation plan.	_____	_____
19. All dangerous supplies out of the children's reach.	_____	_____
20. Classroom set up properly.	_____	_____

The following words of child safety should be
discussed with your child:

Danger: indicates a hazardous situation.

Warning: indicates a possible or impending danger,
problem, or unpleasant situation.

Caution: indicates danger or mistakes.

SAFETY is a as fascinating as "A" "B" "C's"
(always be careful)

Parents, are you aware of more safety rules?
Let's see . . . . WHAT ARE THEY????

Fire Drills

Code Red Drills

9-1-1 for help (and what to say?)

Lock Down

One safety "tip" I offer you is: "make sure you know where your child is at all times."

AND.... that your child knows:

a. Their name, address, and phone number.

If they get lost, tell them to stay where they are.
Don't share
address and phone number if they feel
uncomfortable.

b. NOT to eat anything given to them by a stranger.

c. NEVER go anywhere with a stranger.

> *"Strangers may be danger,*
> *Even if they seem nice.*
> *Stay away from strangers,*
> *When you do not know them.*
> *When a stranger says, "Do not yell."*
> *Yell real loud and run to tell.*
> *When a stranger asks you to come,*
> *Yell! Run! Go tell mommy and daddy!"*
> (Roger W. Hancock)

d. DON'T play with exterminators or fire.

e. DON'T walk away from your porch or yard alone.

.

f. No one is allowed to touch you anywhere on your body.

> *When a person touches me,*
> *In a way that does not feel right to me,*
> *I will say "No! This is my body!"*
> *Then I'll go and tell somebody.*
> *I'll tell and tell, 'til somebody believes me.*
> *'Cause I know, "This is my, body!"*
> (Roger W. Hancock)

91

Hazards in childcare centers cannot be taken lightly. Keeping the children and staff safe is a key responsibility overall. Here are a few common hazards to be aware of:

a. Burns
b. Chemical Bottles within reach of the children.
c. Lifting or carrying children.
d. Poisonings
e. Tripping or Slipping
f. Unplugged Outlets

Parents, I know you don't want to put your child's life at risk because of basic safety procedures and practices not being followed at your child care center. You expect that when you leave your child at the child care center that their level of safety will no longer be a concern. My Kiddie Garden center experienced knee and elbow scratches from our playground, but we were blessed with minimum injuries.

"An ounce of prevention is worth a pound of cure." (Benjamin Franklin)

Some Safety Forms

Used at my Kiddie Garden Center
Issued and required
By the State of New Jersey
For Completion

ACCIDENT/INJURY REPORT The center shall maintain on file a written record of each incident resulting in an injury.	CENTER NAME:		CENTER ADDRESS:	
CHILD'S NAME:	PERSON COMPLETING REPORT:		WITNESS(ES):	
DATE OF INJURY:	TIME OF INJURY:	DATE REPORT COMPLETED:		TIME REPORT COMPLETED:

TYPE OF INJURY: (Check All That Apply)
- [ ] ACHE
- [ ] BITTEN BY ANIMAL
- [ ] BITTEN BY CHILD
- [ ] BITE THAT BROKE THE SKIN
- [ ] BLEEDING
- [ ] BURN
- [ ] BREATHING RAPIDLY
- [ ] OTHER:
- [ ] BREATHING SHALLOW
- [ ] BROKEN BONE SUSPECTED
- [ ] CHOKING
- [ ] CUT
- [ ] DROWSINESS
- [ ] EYE INJURY
- [ ] FALL FROM A HEIGHT OF: ____
- [ ] FOREIGN BODY IN EYE
- [ ] HEAD INJURY
- [ ] ITCHING
- [ ] NAUSEA
- [ ] NOSE BLEED
- [ ] POISIONING
- [ ] RASH
- [ ] REDNESS
- [ ] SCRAPE
- [ ] SCRATCH
- [ ] SPLINTER
- [ ] SPRAIN
- [ ] STING
- [ ] SWELLING

PLACE ON BODY INJURY OCCURRED: (Check All That Apply)
- [ ] ABDOMEN [ ] ARM [ ] ANKLE [ ] BACK [ ] BUTTOCKS
- [ ] CHEEK [ ] CHEST [ ] CHIN [ ] EAR [ ] ELBOW
- [ ] FINGER [ ] FOOT [ ] FOREHEAD [ ] GROIN [ ] HAND
- [ ] HEAD [ ] HIP [ ] KNEE [ ] LEG [ ] LIP
- [ ] MOUTH [ ] NECK [ ] NOSE [ ] SHOULDER [ ] TEETH
- [ ] THIGH [ ] TOE [ ] TONGUE [ ] WRIST
- [ ] OTHER:

WHERE INJURY OCCURRED: (Check All That Apply)
- [ ] CLASSROOM [ ] BATHROOM [ ] SIDEWALK [ ] CAR [ ] FIELD TRIP [ ] KITCHEN
- [ ] HALLWAY [ ] STAIRWAY [ ] PARKING LOT [ ] BUS [ ] PLAYGROUND
- [ ] OTHER:

TYPE OF SURFACE
- [ ] CARPETING [ ] TILE FLOOR [ ] WOOD FLOOR [ ] RUBBER [ ] LAMINATE FLOOR
- [ ] WOOD CHIPS [ ] GRASS [ ] SAND [ ] CONCRETE [ ] ASPHALT
- [ ] OTHER:

DESCRIBE HOW INJURY/ACCIDENT HAPPENED:

TREATMENT/ FOLLOW UP ACTIONS: (Check All That Apply)

FIRST AID GIVEN AT THE CENTER:
- [ ] CLEANED WITH SOAP AND WATER
- [ ] ICE APPLIED
- [ ] ANTISEPTIC APPLIED
- [ ] REST PROVIDED
- [ ] BANDAGE APPLIED
- [ ] CONSOLED CHILD
- [ ] MEDICATION ADMINISTERED:
- [ ] OTHER (DESCRIBE):

STAFF WHO PERFORMED FIRST AID:

OUTSIDE MEDICAL ATTENTION GIVEN:
(Notify the OOL by next working day and provide documentation within 1 week.)
- [ ] AMBULANCE OR 911 CALLED/ONSITE
- [ ] EMERGENCY CARE PROVIDED
- [ ] POISION CONTROL CALLED
- [ ] TRANSPORTED EMERGENCY/URGENT CARE
- [ ] CONSULTATION/TREATMENT BY LICENSED PHYSICIAN OR HEALTH CARE PROVIDER

PARENT NOTIFICATION*:

METHOD OF NOTIFICATION:
- [ ] NOTIFIED BY PHONE [ ] OTHER:
- [ ] NOTIFIED AT PICK UP

TIME OF NOTIFICATION: | COMMENTS:

* Take immediate necessary action to protect the child from further harm and immediately notify the child's parent(s) when a bite breaks the skin; a child sustains a head or facial injury, including when a child bumps his/her head; a child falls from a height greater than the height of the child; or an injury requiring professional medical care occurs.

STAFF SIGNATURE:	DATE:	DIRECTOR SIGNATURE:	DATE:	PARENT SIGNATURE:	DATE:

OOL /3.8.2018

UNUSUAL INCIDENT REPORT

Name of Child:		Date of Incident:	Time of Incident:
Name of Staff Writing Report:		Name of Staff That Notified the Parent:	
Name of Parent:		Date Parent Notified:	

Other Individuals Involved: (i.e. Other Staff/Adults, Witnesses, Children (Described as Child #1, Child #2, etc.)

Name:	Relationship to Child:	Age:	Other Important Information:

Please Indicate, in as Much Detail as Possible, the Incident That Occurred: (Who, What, When, Where, Why, How)

The sponsor, sponsor representative, director, or any staff member shall verbally notify the *State Central Registry Hotline (1-877 NJ ABUSE/1-877-652-2873)* immediately whenever there is reasonable cause to believe that a child has been subjected to abuse or neglect by a staff member, or any other adult. Additionally, the parent(s) shall be notified on the same day of the occurrence of any unusual incident(s) that occurred at the center. Such incidents may include, but are not limited to, unusual sexual activity; violent or destructive behavior; withdrawal or passivity; or significant change(s) in the child's personality, behavior or habits. The center shall maintain on file a record of such incidents and documentation that parents have been informed of them.

Does the nature of this incident indicate abuse or neglect?

NO

YES, the incident was immediately reported to the Child Abuse Hotline at 1-877-NJABUSE (1-877-652-2873)

Name/ID of NJ Abuse Hotline Screener:	Date of Call:	Comments:

Follow-Up Comments and/or Actions (if Needed):

OOL/10.28.2017

Shelter-In-Place/Lockdown* Procedures
If we need to stay in the building due to an emergency, the following procedures will be followed

LOCATION #1 IN CLASSROOMS/BUILDING	LOCATION #2 IN CLASSROOMS/BUILDING

Procedures for Shelter-In-Place/Lockdown	Notification
	EMERGENCY RESPONDERS WILL BE NOTIFIED WHEN
	PARENTS/GUARDIANS WILL BE NOTIFIED WHEN

Emergency Kit

LOCATION(S)	CONTENTS

Parent/Guardian and Child Reunification Procedures
If we need to evacuate, shelter-in-place, or when parents/guardians/guardians are unable to get to children, the following procedures will be followed to reunite children with parents/guardians or designated contacts as soon as it is safe.

Notification
PARENTS/GUARDIANS WILL BE NOTIFIED WHEN

Release of Children
Children will only be released to parents/guardians or other individuals listed on the child's form (with proper ID)

OTHER DETAILS ABOUT REUNIFICATION

Local Enforcement Agency Notifications

	Phone Number:	Contact Person:	Notes:
Law Enforcement (Police)			
Emergency Management			
Fire Department			

Utility Information

	Company Name:	24-Hour Number:	Shut-Off Location:
Gas			
Electric			
Water			

ANNUAL LOG FOR FIRE DRILLS AND LOCKDOWN DRILLS

Center Name:

License ID:

DATE OF DRILL	TIME OF DRILL*	WEATHER	# OF CHILDREN	# OF STAFF	TOTAL TIME TO EVACUATE**	STAFF INITIALS	COMMENTS

LOCKDOWN DRILL # 1	LOCKDOWN DRILL # 2
DATE:	DATE:
COMMENTS:	COMMENTS:

FIRE DRILLS (1 DRILL PER SESSION/PER MONTH)
*One fire drill per year must be conducted during nap time.
**All children present must be evacuated within 3 minutes.
LOCKDOWN DRILLS (2 DRILLS PER SESSION/PER YEAR)

OOL/1.6.2018

98

Evacuation and Relocation Procedures
If we need to evacuate our site and relocate to another site, the following procedures will be followed

EVACUATION ROUTES/EXITS
☑ Center Diagram Attached (includes evacuation routes from each classroom and outdoor play area)

EVACUATING INFANTS/TODDLERS (if applicable)
Describe any special circumstances or procedures needed for evacuating infants and toddlers from the building.

EVACUATING CHILDREN WITH DISABILITIES OR CHRONIC MEDICAL CONDITIONS (if applicable)
Describe any special circumstances or procedures needed for evacuating children with disabilities or chronic medical conditions from the building including procedures for storing a child's medically necessary medicine.

Procedures for Evacuation	Notification
	EMERGENCY RESPONDERS WILL BE NOTIFIED WHEN
	PARENTS/GUARDIANS WILL BE NOTIFIED WHEN

Emergency Kit
LOCATION(S)	CONTENTS

Evacuation Locations

On-Site Evacuation Location (i.e. fire drills, very short time period of displacement)

ON-SITE LOCATION	ALTERNATE ON-SITE LOCATION

Off-Site (Indoor) Evacuation Location (i.e. gas leak, fire, any center displacement for an extended period of time)

OFF-SITE (INDOOR) EVACUATION LOCATION		ALTERNATE OFF-SITE (INDOOR) EVACUATION LOCATION	
Building Name		Building Name	
Street Address	City	Street Address	City
Phone Number	Contact Name	Phone Number	Contact Name
Other Details		Other Details	

☐ Operates during the same operating hours as the center.
☐ Location is within safe walking distance.
☐ Transportation required. See "Emergency Transportation" above.

☐ Operates during the same operating hours as the center.
☐ Location is within safe walking distance.
☐ Transportation required. See "Emergency Transportation" above.

OOL; 10.26.2017

CHAPTER 9

Parents Your Child's Health Matters

Parents, are you aware that your child's greatest wealth is their *health*? Their health is a very serious challenge because their little bodies, minds, spirits, and souls should be aligned with God's design. Your child's body is holy and needs to be taken care of. Parents, please take care of your child's health. It is not an occasional thought of action, but a routine that is as important as eating wholesome food on a daily basis. Regular doctor visits for your child are important also, but the majority of what shapes their health depends on circumstances outside the doctor's office. They include conditions where your child lives, what your child learns, and how your child plays and has fun.

Parents, you can adopt the following "Healthy Habits Pledge," and please be honest to share and follow with your child to make this a daily routine which can be the best start in their life:

I pledge to stay healthy and clean
through exercise and good hygiene,

I will eat a balanced meal every day
to have more energy to learn and play.

Every night I will get a good rest
to be more ready to do my best!

If I work hard to be healthy and strong,
I'll be happier my whole life long.

I call your attention also to the fact that your child is more likely to catch many contagious illnesses. However, most mild health issues can and should be treated at home. We advocated at my Kiddie Garden center that if your child is sick, "please keep them at home" and return to the center with a doctor's note indicating that your child is now well to return to the center. Social distancing was also practiced at Kiddie Garden as well as the teaching of effective hand-washing techniques. Additionally, no touching of their face or other surfaces like their bed at bedtime, nap time, play time, and outdoors. With basic health care, successful early learning can be achieved.

However, even with your best intentions, your child is exposed to germs every day.

Germs, germs, everywhere,

On your hands and in your hair.

Wash your hands every time,

After bathroom, after playtime.

Even on toys you share,

Germs are hiding everywhere.

Wash your hands all the time,

Especially before, dinner time.

There are usually additional signs of more serious illnesses. So, if and when your child has a temperature <u>over</u> 100 degrees, you will be called and asked to pick up your child and take him/her home.

The licensing policy by New Jersey regarding "health" promotes very good practices for the children attending a childcare center. This policy regarding your child's illnesses protects them from serious harm. The bottom line is making sure that your child has a healthy mind, body, and soul.

Parents, there are some "new health" issues that are <u>alarming;</u> obesity, risky adolescent behavior disorders, depression, and the need for guidance education, but I will focus on OBESITY because it's the leading health issue right now among our young children, and the fact that it has doubled. In some cases; it has even tripled within the last three decades. This particular health issue is a challenge due to unhealthy diets, many liquid calories, and inactivity. Parents, this occurs in young children which is why good nutrition, proper sleep, and exercise are so important. Oh yes, obesity will affect academic achievement. Do you find what was just said to be evident about your child? Well, whatca' gonna' do about this??????

Obesity!

I wonder how you came to be.
You now have control over me,
A healthy life I cannot see.

A little added here and there,
And now the people seem to stare.
This weight my bones can barely bear,
I'll change my ways, but do I dare?

Less sugar, less salt – that I know,
And a walk each day – start out slow.
Make healthy choices as I go,
Learn it's okay to just say no.

Make lifetime changes carefully,
My weight will change naturally.
(Bill Baker)

"Change your child's choices and their health and the length of their lives will be normal and happy."

Parents, your child should be encouraged to do a variety of activities and exercises with different challenges within the day.

It is suggested that these activities and exercises be carried out 3 hours daily:

Active play with other children.

Riding their tricycle or bicycle.

Throwing and catching.

As well as activities that involve:

Hopping, skipping or tumbling.

Dancing.

Create a healthy smile.

Guidelines For Good Sleep

Age	Time
4 months–12 months	12 to 16 hours
1 – 2 years	11 to 14 hours
3 – 5 years	10 to 13 hours
6 – 12 years	9 to 12 hours
13 – 18 years	8 to 10 hours

Practice <u>healthy eating habits.</u>

Food listings can be found in "Growing Great Minds II' 'Chapter 9 'Yummies for the Tiny Tummies'

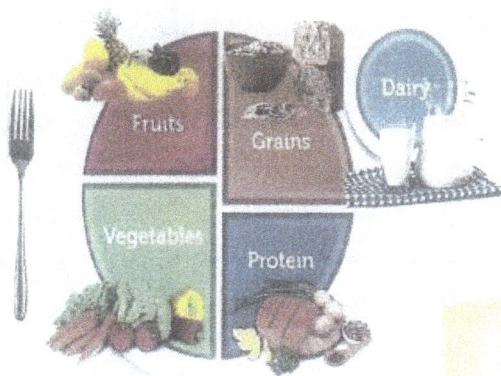

Take your child to the dentist. In the meantime, have your child <u>Brush and Floss</u> daily.

Plan to help your child reach their milestones which are critical to their future success.

Your child's "HEALTH MATTERS" because it will provide the foundation for any and all future LEARNING, BEHAVIOR, and "HEALTH" to become a future diligent adult.

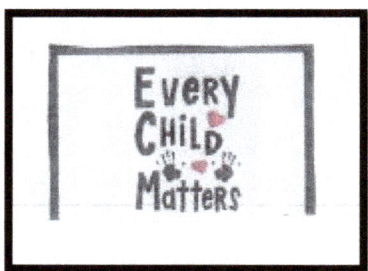

Some Health Forms

Used at my Kiddie Garden Center
Issued and required
by the State of New Jersey
For Completion

APPENDIX H

UNIVERSAL
CHILD HEALTH RECORD

Endorsed by: American Academy of Pediatrics, New Jersey Chapter
New Jersey Academy of Family Physicians
New Jersey Department of Health

SECTION I - TO BE COMPLETED BY PARENT(S)			
Child's Name *(Last)*	*(First)*	Gender ☐ Male ☐ Female	Date of Birth / /
Does Child Have Health Insurance? ☐ Yes ☐ No	If Yes, Name of Child's Health Insurance Carrier		
Parent/Guardian Name	Home Telephone Number ( ) -	Work Telephone/Cell Phone Number ( ) -	
Parent/Guardian Name	Home Telephone Number ( ) -	Work Telephone/Cell Phone Number ( ) -	

I give my consent for my child's Health Care Provider and Child Care Provider/School Nurse to discuss the information on this form.

Signature/Date	This form may be released to WIC. ☐ Yes ☐ No

SECTION II - TO BE COMPLETED BY HEALTH CARE PROVIDER	
Date of Physical Examination:	Results of physical examination normal? ☐ Yes ☐ No

Abnormalities Noted:		
	Weight *(must be taken within 30 days for WIC)*	
	Height *(must be taken within 30 days for WIC)*	
	Head Circumference *(If <2 Years)*	
	Blood Pressure *(If ≥3 Years)*	

IMMUNIZATIONS	☐ Immunization Record Attached ☐ Date Next Immunization Due:

MEDICAL CONDITIONS

Chronic Medical Conditions/Related Surgeries • List medical conditions/ongoing surgical concerns:	☐ None ☐ Special Care Plan Attached	Comments
Medications/Treatments • List medications/treatments:	☐ None ☐ Special Care Plan Attached	Comments
Limitations to Physical Activity • List limitations/special considerations:	☐ None ☐ Special Care Plan Attached	Comments
Special Equipment Needs • List items necessary for daily activities	☐ None ☐ Special Care Plan Attached	Comments
Allergies/Sensitivities • List allergies:	☐ None ☐ Special Care Plan Attached	Comments
Special Diet/Vitamin & Mineral Supplements • List dietary specifications:	☐ None ☐ Special Care Plan Attached	Comments
Behavioral Issues/Mental Health Diagnosis • List behavioral/mental health issues/concerns:	☐ None ☐ Special Care Plan Attached	Comments
Emergency Plans • List emergency plan that might be needed and the sign/symptoms to watch for:	☐ None ☐ Special Care Plan Attached	Comments

PREVENTIVE HEALTH SCREENINGS

Type Screening	Date Performed	Record Value	Type Screening	Date Performed	Note If Abnormal
Hgb/Hct			Hearing		
Lead: ☐ Capillary ☐ Venous			Vision		
TB (mm of Induration)			Dental		
Other:			Developmental		
Other:			Scoliosis		

☐ *I have examined the above student and reviewed his/her health history. It is my opinion that he/she is medically cleared to participate fully in all child care/school activities, including physical education and competitive contact sports, unless noted above.*

Name of Health Care Provider (Print)	Health Care Provider Stamp:
Signature/Date	

DH-14   OCT 17   Distribution: Original-Child Care Provider   Copy-Parent/Guardian   Copy-Health Care Provider

ILLNESS LOG

For the documentation of illnesses, symptoms of illness, or diseases that are exhibited by each child while in the center's care and the exclusion of children as a result of the COVID-19 daily health screening. This log may be used to document COVID-19 related staff exclusions.

NAME	☐ CHILD ☐ STAFF	DATE	TIME	DATE REMOVED	DATE RETURNED

SYMPTOMS (CHECK ALL THAT APPLY)
☐ Cough ☐ Fever ☐ COVID-19 Symptoms[2]
☐ Diarrhea ☐ Nausea/Vomiting
☐ Difficulty Breathing ☐ Pain/Discomfort
☐ Eye Redness/Discharge ☐ Rash/Ringworm
☐ Other:

RESPONSE ACTIONS (CHECK ALL THAT APPLY)
☐ Rested at Center ☐ Emergency Medical Care Provided[1]
☐ Child Picked Up
☐ Denied Entry[2] ☐ Health Department Notified
☐ Called 911[1]
☐ Other:

READMITTED BASED ON (CHECK ALL THAT APPLY)
☐ Health Care Provider Note
☐ Symptom-Free
☐ Isolation/Quarantine Complete
☐ COVID-19 Negative Result
☐ Other:

NAME	☐ CHILD ☐ STAFF	DATE	TIME	DATE REMOVED	DATE RETURNED

SYMPTOMS (CHECK ALL THAT APPLY)
☐ Cough ☐ Fever ☐ COVID-19 Symptoms[2]
☐ Diarrhea ☐ Nausea/Vomiting
☐ Difficulty Breathing ☐ Pain/Discomfort
☐ Eye Redness/Discharge ☐ Rash/Ringworm
☐ Other:

RESPONSE ACTIONS (CHECK ALL THAT APPLY)
☐ Rested at Center ☐ Emergency Medical Care Provided[1]
☐ Child Picked Up
☐ Denied Entry[2] ☐ Health Department Notified
☐ Called 911[1]
☐ Other:

READMITTED BASED ON (CHECK ALL THAT APPLY)
☐ Health Care Provider Note
☐ Symptom-Free
☐ Isolation/Quarantine Complete
☐ COVID-19 Negative Result
☐ Other:

NAME	☐ CHILD ☐ STAFF	DATE	TIME	DATE REMOVED	DATE RETURNED

SYMPTOMS (CHECK ALL THAT APPLY)
☐ Cough ☐ Fever ☐ COVID-19 Symptoms[2]
☐ Diarrhea ☐ Nausea/Vomiting
☐ Difficulty Breathing ☐ Pain/Discomfort
☐ Eye Redness/Discharge ☐ Rash/Ringworm
☐ Other:

RESPONSE ACTIONS (CHECK ALL THAT APPLY)
☐ Rested at Center ☐ Emergency Medical Care Provided[1]
☐ Child Picked Up
☐ Denied Entry[2] ☐ Health Department Notified
☐ Called 911[1]
☐ Other:

READMITTED BASED ON (CHECK ALL THAT APPLY)
☐ Health Care Provider Note
☐ Symptom-Free
☐ Isolation/Quarantine Complete
☐ COVID-19 Negative Result
☐ Other:

NAME	☐ CHILD ☐ STAFF	DATE	TIME	DATE REMOVED	DATE RETURNED

SYMPTOMS (CHECK ALL THAT APPLY)
☐ Cough ☐ Fever ☐ COVID-19 Symptoms[2]
☐ Diarrhea ☐ Nausea/Vomiting
☐ Difficulty Breathing ☐ Pain/Discomfort
☐ Eye Redness/Discharge ☐ Rash/Ringworm
☐ Other:

RESPONSE ACTIONS (CHECK ALL THAT APPLY)
☐ Rested at Center ☐ Emergency Medical Care Provided[1]
☐ Child Picked Up
☐ Denied Entry[2] ☐ Health Department Notified
☐ Called 911[1]
☐ Other:

READMITTED BASED ON (CHECK ALL THAT APPLY)
☐ Health Care Provider Note
☐ Symptom-Free
☐ Isolation/Quarantine Complete
☐ COVID-19 Negative Result
☐ Other:

NAME	☐ CHILD ☐ STAFF	DATE	TIME	DATE REMOVED	DATE RETURNED

SYMPTOMS (CHECK ALL THAT APPLY)
☐ Cough ☐ Fever ☐ COVID-19 Symptoms[2]
☐ Diarrhea ☐ Nausea/Vomiting
☐ Difficulty Breathing ☐ Pain/Discomfort
☐ Eye Redness/Discharge ☐ Rash/Ringworm
☐ Other:

RESPONSE ACTIONS (CHECK ALL THAT APPLY)
☐ Rested at Center ☐ Emergency Medical Care Provided[1]
☐ Child Picked Up
☐ Denied Entry[2] ☐ Health Department Notified
☐ Called 911[1]
☐ Other:

READMITTED BASED ON (CHECK ALL THAT APPLY)
☐ Health Care Provider Note
☐ Symptom-Free
☐ Isolation/Quarantine Complete
☐ COVID-19 Negative Result
☐ Other:

NAME	☐ CHILD ☐ STAFF	DATE	TIME	DATE REMOVED	DATE RETURNED

SYMPTOMS (CHECK ALL THAT APPLY)
☐ Cough ☐ Fever ☐ COVID-19 Symptoms[2]
☐ Diarrhea ☐ Nausea/Vomiting
☐ Difficulty Breathing ☐ Pain/Discomfort
☐ Eye Redness/Discharge ☐ Rash/Ringworm
☐ Other:

RESPONSE ACTIONS (CHECK ALL THAT APPLY)
☐ Rested at Center ☐ Emergency Medical Care Provided[1]
☐ Child Picked Up
☐ Denied Entry[2] ☐ Health Department Notified
☐ Called 911[1]
☐ Other:

READMITTED BASED ON (CHECK ALL THAT APPLY)
☐ Health Care Provider Note
☐ Symptom-Free
☐ Isolation/Quarantine Complete
☐ COVID-19 Negative Result
☐ Other:

---

[1] Centers must report to the OOL by the next working day and submit documentation through NJCCIS within one week when an illness results in a call to 911, a child visiting the emergency room or being admitted to the hospital, or a child receiving on-site or transported emergency care/urgent care. Refer to Reporting Requirements for Communicable Diseases and Work-Related Conditions Quick Reference guide at http://www.nj.gov/health/cd/documents/reportable_disease_magnet.pdf.

[2] Staff and/or children exhibiting COVID-19 symptoms must be denied entry/immediately excluded. Positive cases of COVID-19 must be immediately reported to the local health department and the OOL.

OOL/05.26.2021

MEDICAL DECLARATION STATEMENT FOR SCHOOL-AGE CHILD CARE
(AND/OR FOR CHILDREN ENROLLED IN PUBLIC OR PRIVATE SCHOOL)

CHILD'S NAME:	DATE OF BIRTH:	GRADE IN SEPTEMBER:

HEALTH STATEMENT (CHECK ONE)

☐ My child is in good health and can participate in the normal activities of the program and has no conditions or special needs that require special accommodations.

☐ My child can participate in the normal activities of the program but has conditions or special needs that require special accommodations as indicated below.

SCHOOL-AGE CHILD'S SPECIAL CONDITIONS OR NEEDS REQUIRING SPECIAL ACCOMMODATIONS

Please list any allergies, medical conditions, including chronic health problems (such as asthma, seizures), behavioral disorders, special needs, etc.

PARENT/GUARDIAN SIGNATURE:	DATE:

OOL/10.21.2017

113

Conclusion

I wrote this book with concern about the importance and effects of parental involvement through engagement, to seek out long-term success, and to develop a life-long 'love' of learning while on their child's educational journey – not only in school, but at home as well. And it is not only important, but <u>necessary</u> to be involved within <u>all</u> aspects of your child's life. "Education is not preparation for life; education is life itself" (John Dewey).

I realize that parenting can be very hard, but it is also very rewarding. The crappy part is that the reward comes much later than the hard work. Also, that there is no such thing as a "perfect" parent.

You are to be reminded of how quickly the years go by and that your child's undertakings change every day. They are so ready to learn and grow, and you will be surprised at just how much they know. It's a challenge. Are you ready? MEET THE CHALLENGE!

You will find that many of the children have their own personalities, likes, dislikes, facial expressions, and the list goes on and on. But through it all, it teaches you as a parent, the real meaning of unconditional love.

"Growing Great Minds III" features parent responsibility, support, and involvement." Parent responsibility is for you to 'do your part' when it comes to <u>your</u> child. In other words, take reasonable <u>care</u> of them. Also, remember to use the 4 'P's of strategies of care, which are: to be passionate, perspective, purposeful, and progressive.

"Let us sacrifice our today so that our children can have a better tomorrow." (A.P.J. Abdul Kalam)

Parents should also support their child in many ways. Namely in effective learning support, by listening to their concerns, praising them, and ensuring continuity in learning. *"I love my parents in the way most children would: for having been there at every point in my youth and childhood, ready to pick me up when I fell and <u>support</u> me when I stumble"* (Michael Gove).

<u>Involvement</u> calls for the participation of parents in their role in educational activities. *"Behind the child that makes the most progress is an actively involved parent."* (Pinterest)

"Your children need your <u>presence</u>, not your <u>presents</u>. (Jesse Jackson)

I humbly conclude with the attached prayer and Bible verse with the hopes that it will have a positive outcome for you.

> "All our children shall be taught by the Lord and great will be their peace, their health, safety, protection, and prosperity."

> Isaiah 54:13-14

A PARENT'S PRAYER

*O **Heavenly Father**, make me a better parent. Teach me to understand my children, to listen patiently to what they have to say, and to answer all their questions kindly. Keep me from interrupting them or contradicting them. Make me as courteous to them as I would have them be to me.*

Forbid that I should ever laugh at their mistakes or resort to shame or ridicule when they displease me. May I never punish them for my own selfish satisfaction or to show my power.

Let me not tempt my child to lie or steal. And guide me hour by hour that I may demonstrate by all I say and do that honesty produces happiness.

Reduce, I pray, the meanness in me. And when I am out of sorts, help me, O Lord, to hold my tongue.

May I ever be mindful that my children are children, and I should not expect of them the judgment of adults.

Let me not rob them of the opportunity to wait on themselves and to make decisions.

Bless me with the generosity to grant them all their reasonable requests and the courage to deny them privileges I know will do them harm.

Make me fair and just and kind. Help me, O Lord, to be loved and respected and imitated by my children. Amen. (Janelle Nehrenz)

ABOUT THE AUTHOR

Dr. *Elaine S. McGhee* has served in the field of education for over fifty years. She received her high school diploma from Southside High School (currently Shabazz High School) in Newark, N.J., her B.S. Commerce Degree from Rider University in Trenton, N.J., M.A. Degree from Jersey City State (currently New Jersey City University) in Jersey City, N.J., Student Personnel Services Certificate from Montclair State (currently Montclair University) in Montclair, New Jersey, Doctor of Education from Nova Southeastern University in Fort Lauderdale, Florida.

Dr. McGhee has more teaching, guidance counseling, and administrative experiences that are not currently included in this bio. However, she is available as a consultant based on her experience in most educational settings.

A retired educator, Dr. McGhee served as an elementary and secondary school teacher, Guidance Counselor, and Administrator in Essex, Hudson, and Union Counties. She has also served as Supervisor of Pupil Personnel Services, Essex County Professor, Seton Hall University

Upward Bound Associate Director, Project GRAD Newark College Scholarship Manager and Director of her own facility, "Kiddie Garden Child Care" (closed due to COVID-19).

Her present-day vision as she looks at her two adult children, Darren and Elissa, and her only adult granddaughter, Shaniah, is to continue to serve as a guide to assist in providing wisdom, a sense of purpose, and most of all **LOVE.** She carried them in her arms when they were young, but now she carries them in her heart. Uniqueness is what makes them so beautiful and special to her and she will continue to smile because she knows how wonderfully blessed she is.

Parents, here is a word search game for you

Have

A

Little

<u>FUN</u>

too!

Childcare Word Search

Using the secret code, can you find the hidden word?

1 = j	10 = f	19 = s
2 = d	11 = b	20 = e
3 = y	12 = q	21 = w
4 = p	13 = x	22 = n
5 = a	14 = o	23 = c
6 = r	15 = h	24 = t
7 = m	16 = l	25 = k
8 = z	17 = u	26 = g
9 = v	18 = i	

4 16 5 3

5 17 2 18 24 14 6 3

4 6 20 19 23 15 14 14 16 20

5 6 18 24 15 7 20 24 18 23

18 22 19 4 18 6 20

6 20 5 2 18 22 26

11 20 5 17 24 18 10 17 16

"Don't Peak"

WORDS

Arithmetic   *Play*

Auditory   *Preschool*

Beautiful   *Reading*

Inspire

ORDER INFORMATION

You can order additional copies of this book by emailing the author directly using the email address below.

Dr. Elaine S. McGhee

Email Address: eeartdr@aol.com

Books are available at Amazon.com, BN.com Kindle and Your Local Bookstores (By Request)

Please leave a review for this book on Amazon and let other readers know how much you enjoyed reading it.

Thank you!